How Great Is Your Gal?

How Great Is Your Gal?

SARAH CHRISTENSEN FU
ILLUSTRATIONS BY
KATIE ABEY

This book is dedicated to
my wonderful husband, Andrew Fu.

Text © Sarah Christensen Fu 2017
Illustrations by Katie Abey
Cover and interior design:
Rosamund Saunders
Cover images © Shutterstock

Skyhorse Publishing books may be purchased in bulk at special discounts for sales promotion, corporate gifts, fund-raising, or educational purposes. Special editions can also be created to specifications. For details, contact the Special Sales Department, Skyhorse Publishing, 307 West 36th Street, 11th Floor, New York, NY 10018 or info@skyhorsepublishing.com.

Visit our website at www.skyhorsepublishing.com.

10 9 8 7 6 5 4 3 2 1

Library of Congress Cataloging-in-Publication Data is available on file.

ISBN: 978-1-5107-2128-9

Printed in China

FSC™ is a nonprofit international organization established to promote the responsible management of the world's forests. Products carrying the FSC label are independently certified to assure consumers that they come from forests that are managed to meet the social, economic, and ecological needs of present and future generations.

Contents

Introduction

Today's modern woman wears many hats, and she can flip the switch from a bulldog in the boardroom to a cheerleader at a child's sporting event, then, if you're lucky, effortlessly slide into the role of bedroom vixen.

It's true: today's woman isn't just satisfied to "have it all." She wants to have it all right now! Multitasking is at an all-time high, with apps and social media and spreadsheets and yoga class and never being able to turn it off. To really get to know your woman, you need to cut through all of life's day-to-day noise in order to see her true personality.

The right partner can change your life, and when you and your partner are in sync, she'll be your best friend, playmate, hot date, and muse. When assessing your life partner, it's important to be able to look objectively—past her curves and charms, ambition and creativity—and evaluate her character traits, along with her physical and mental capabilities.

Is your woman queen of the kitchen? Is she a master of mathematics, a dancefloor diva, a literary genius, a multitasking marvel? And while she's doing all these things, does she still make time to prioritize her mate's needs—does she remember your favorite foods, distant family members, and cherished childhood stuffed animal?

This book contains a series of tests and activities designed for you to get to the bottom of your woman's complexities, and to help you gather data in key categories so you can understand how to deal with the woman of your dreams—and avoid making a misstep that will turn your happy life into a nightmare!

Chapter One

The Cool Quotient

She may be brilliant, beautiful, and bold, but does your gal have the cool factor? That certain *je ne sais quoi* that allows her to hang out with your friends, kill it at work, and fit in with your family—even your grumpy grandpa.

1 She's Cool With It

Does your gal stay cool under pressure? Which of these things would your gal legitimately be cool with? Award her 1 point for each rude, mean, or careless thing that would not make her bat an eyelid.

You accidentally stay out all night. ☐

You burp or fart in public. ☐

You break an heirloom that her grandmother gave her. ☐

You change the channel in the middle of her show. ☐

You eat the leftover dessert and don't share any with her. ☐

You unplug her phone from the charger and forget to plug it back in. ☐

You don't text back right away. ☐

You leave your dirty clothes all over the floor. ☐

You forget to use a coaster on the coffee table. ☐

You are half an hour late to dinner with her parents. ☐

Total Score ____ (0–10 pts)

2 Hell Hath No Fury

Just how scary is your woman when she is frustrated? Does she whine like a puppy when something goes wrong, or charge like an angry rhino at the smallest infraction? Rate her level of anger in terms of these animal sounds.

She roars like a lion and scratches like one too.

NIL POINTS

You can tell she's mad because she rattles like a rattlesnake. If you don't get out of the way in time, you'll get a deadly bite.

1 POINT

She sounds like a parrot, repeating the same things over and over again. 2 POINTS

She barks at you, but plays nice again as soon as you fall into line. 3 POINTS

She just purrs. Your woman has trained you well enough to keep her happy. 4 POINTS

Total Score ____ (0–4 pts)

3 Common Interests

One of the coolest things about having a cool gal is being able to share hobbies and get excited about the same stuff. Award her 1 point for each of the following interests and hobbies you both share (feel free to substitute your own unique interests for anything on this list).

Professional sports. ☐

Latest tech gadgets. ☐

Online trends. ☐

Extreme sports. ☐

Action movies. ☐

Military history. ☐

Craft beer. ☐

Superheroes. ☐

Comic books. ☐

Cars. ☐

Total Score ____ (0–10 pts)

4 Sweet as Pie

Give your gal points for each sweet thing she does on the list below. If she does it rarely, give her 1 point; if she does it sometimes, give her 2 points; if she does it often—that's a 3-pointer!

	RARELY (1 pt)	SOMETIMES (2 pts)	OFTEN (3 pts)
Cooks something you like			
Makes you your favorite after-work drink			
Plans a date night that you'll love			
Relaxes at home with you instead of always being busy			
Lets your less-than-perfect behavior slide			
Stays with you (if you're still together, give her 3 points)			

Total Score _____ (0–18 pts)

Chapter One: Scoring

Add up your score on each question to get your total score for Chapter One, then find out how your woman measures up below.

Q1 Score ____ (0–10 pts)

Q2 Score ____ (0–4 pts)

Q3 Score ____ (0–10 pts)

Q4 Score ____ (0–18 pts)

Total Chapter Score ___ (0–42 pts)

32–42 pts: Your gal is the coolest. She's got your back, she loves you, and she loves your life together. Go give her a high-five.

20–31 pts: Your gal is pretty darn cool. She's got standards, she's got her own life and has expectations of you—but she goes out of her way to make sure you feel respected and get to have lots of fun. You understand one another, and good communication is what makes a relationship tick.

10–19 pts: Your woman keeps you honest, admit it. She doesn't let you get away with everything, but she is cool when it really counts. Focus on the good stuff and just leave her to it if she freaks out about something. She'll eventually tire herself out and then come in for a cuddle.

0–9 pts: Relationships can get weird when one partner acts like the "parent" and the other acts like the "child"—and sometimes couples get into cycles that are tough to break. If your gal isn't being cool to you, try being cooler to her for a while and see if it changes things for the better.

Chapter Two

The Social Situation

Women tend to have friends. Sometimes those friends are great. Sometimes they're out of their mind. Sometimes they're over at your house, eating all your food. Sometimes they're texting or messaging and filling your house with those little dings and beeps. Sometimes they make your gal happy and sometimes they drive her completely batty. Test your partner on her social situation and see how she scores.

1 BFFs

Lifelong friends are great for stability and show a sense of loyalty. Can your woman hang on to friends forever, or is there a constantly rotating cast of characters parading through your life? Which of these best describes her friends?

Friends? She tolerates new acquaintances until they annoy her. **NIL POINTS**

She has had at least one friend for more than a year.
1 POINT

She has a few friends, but they have very little in common and don't seem to like each other that much—at least until they start drinking. **2 POINTS**

She has a core group of friends, but they seem to shift allegiances on a regular basis. Keeping up with them is like keeping up with a soap opera. **3 POINTS**

She has long-term friends that bring out the best in her, and they genuinely enjoy each other's company.
4 POINTS

Total Score _____ (0–4 pts)

2 Do Not Disturb!

Your gal's friends, acquaintances, and cohorts have her phone number—and you better believe they use it. But just because they call, does she have to answer? Give your girl 1 point for each situation in which she would either turn her phone off or silence it instead of answering or texting back.

Church. ☐

Date night. ☐

Work. ☐

Doctor's office. ☐

Movie theater. ☐

Family get-together. ☐

Sporting event. ☐

Gym. ☐

Restaurant. ☐

Public transportation. ☐

Total Score _____ (0–10 pts)

3 Under the Influence

Girls just wanna have fun—but do they actually have fun? When your gal spends time with her friends, does she come home happy and refreshed, or annoyed, confused, and possibly inebriated? Choose the description that best describes your partner when she comes home from hanging out with her friends.

Angry, swearing, jealous, deranged, and possibly drunk. NIL POINTS

Gossipy, nitpicky, and generally cross. She always says this is the last time she'll see so-and-so. 1 POINT

Seems a little riled up but says she had fun. 2 POINTS

Smiling, relieved to be home with you, and maybe even a little cuddly. 3 POINTS

Inspired and delighted by her friends and excited to share the details with you. 4 POINTS

Total Score ____ (0–4 pts)

4 Activity: The Friend Facts of Life

Remembering what is happening in a friend's life is one of the primary duties of female friendship. Can your girl keep up with her old friend from school, Katie, who is in town for a few days? Read the following statement quickly to your partner, and then quiz her on which details she remembers. Award her 1 point for each item she recalls correctly.

Your best friend Katie came over to visit. Katie lives in New York, but she used to live in London. Her ex-husband Michael was supposed to have her kids at a beach house, but he let her down because his new girlfriend Bella stubbed her toe or something (actually, she broke her foot while training for a marathon—ugh!). Anyway, Katie asked you if you can watch her children: Jasmine is twelve, Luke is eight, and the baby is, well, a baby. Jasmine has to go to a school concert at 7P.M. on 9th Avenue and needs to practice after school, and Luke is going to a birthday party at 9A.M. on Jones Street. Katie has to go to a job interview at 10A.M. Luke needs a lunch but can't bring anything with peanuts, and Jasmine will need her French horn. The baby's teething toy is shaped like a giraffe and buried in the diaper bag, and he'll start crying like crazy without it if Jasmine starts practicing.

Where does Katie live now?

How did Katie's ex-husband's girlfriend injure herself?

What is Katie's ex-husband's girlfriend's name?

How old is Luke?

What instrument does Jasmine play?

What animal is the baby's teething toy shaped like?

What street is Jasmine's school concert on?

What is the baby's name?

What kind of lunch should you make for Luke?

When is Katie's interview?

Total Score ___ (0–10 pts)

Answers: New York, Broke her foot, Bella, Eight, French Horn, Giraffe, 9th Avenue, Not given, Something without peanuts, 10 A.M.

Chapter Two: Scoring

Add up your score on each question to get your total score for Chapter Two, then find out how your woman measures up below.

Q1 Score ___ (0–4 pts)

Q2 Score ___ (0–10 pts)

Q3 Score ___ (0–4 pts)

Q4 Score ___ (0–10 pts)

Total Chapter Score ___ (0–28 pts)

21–28 pts: Your gal has great taste in friends and balances her healthy friendships with her relationship and other obligations. Her friends respect and appreciate her, and she prides herself on being a good friend to them as well.

14–20 pts: Your gal may fantasize about having a group of friends like those in *Sex and the City* or a rom-com movie, but when her real, human friends don't quite live up to her fictional ideal, she gets frustrated and annoyed. If she can let go of the fantasy, she'll realize she actually likes her friends!

7–13 pts: Your woman loves her pals, but sometimes her social life gets a little out of balance. She may feel pressure to keep up with her friends, or compete with them when it comes to career achievements, kids, exercise, nutrition, or any of the other areas where women can get a little cutthroat.

0–6 pts: Your girl sees her friends more like colleagues—whether the job is PTO, get-togethers, big nights out, or charity work. She probably needs to drop the pals that make her miserable and find some kindred spirits. But you can't tell her that, so just be there to hug her or hold her hair back when she returns from seeing them.

Chapter Three

Beauty Business

The beauty business is very important to some women, much less important to others—and usually least important to very young ladies and those blessed with naturally good looks. While highlights, lowlights, hair relaxers, hair curlers, hair extensions, hair clips, headbands, and hats can all add to a woman's beauty, the expense can add up! Does your woman walk the line between looking lovely and going for broke?

1 Beauty Takes Time

How long does your gal usually spend getting ready for a night out with you at a reasonably fancy place? You're not dining with the Queen, but does your woman go all-out princess for any occasion?

She never actually finishes. After about an hour she may leave the bathroom, but she's primping, freshening up, and looking in the mirror all night long. **NIL POINTS**

She spends at least an hour in the bathroom and uses more devices, tubes, creams, and colors than a professional.

1 POINT

The amount of time she spends doesn't matter—she complains about how she looks and begs for compliments no matter what. **2 POINTS**

She spends just enough time to look great every time, but has a hard time believing how good she looks.

3 POINTS

She spends just enough time to look great every time, and she knows it. **4 POINTS**

Total Score ____ (0–4 pts)

2 Presto Chango

Remember the way your girl looked on your first date? That was a good look, right? TV shows, celebrity makeovers, and advertisements encourage ladies to change their look more often than their underwear.

Look back at pictures from when you started dating and award your girl 1 point for each thing on this list that she hasn't changed since you first fell in love.

Hairstyle. ☐

Hair color. ☐

Sense of humor. ☐

Fashion choices. ☐

Shoes. ☐

Makeup. ☐

Tattoos and piercings. ☐

Eyebrows. ☐

Taste in jewelry. ☐

Lingerie style. ☐

Total Score ____ (0–10 pts)

3 The Secret Ingredient

Your gal may use a lot of beauty products each day, but does she really know what's in them? Ask her to match the crazy ingredient in the left-hand column with the everyday beauty product on the right, and award 1 point for each correct match.

1. Lanolin (grease from the fur of sheep)

2. Fish scales

3. Beetles

4. Snail slime

a. High-end face cream

b. Red lipstick

c. Lotions, makeup removers, lipsticks

d. Shimmery lipstick and makeup

Total Score ____ (0–4 pts)

Answers: 1c, 2d, 3b, 4a

4 Activity: Beauty Product Bingo

Does your woman have too many beauty products? Spend a few moments in your bathroom and play a quick game of BINGO! Place a tick on any of the products you see. You shout BINGO and award 1 point when you get a line down, across, or diagonally.

Part 1:

Nail varnish	Hair brush	Face wash	Lipstick	Makeup brush
Comb	Bubble bath	Facial peel	Shower gel	BB cream
Body moisturiser	Hair conditioner	Blush	Mascara	Fake eyelashes
Lip pencil	Face moisturiser	Eye shadow	Shampoo	Anything with glitter
Eye liner	Eyelash curler	Concealer	Base	Fake tan

Total Score ____ (0–12 pts)

Part 2:

Some women have a tendency to fill drawers or boxes with makeup that they never use. Is your girl a beauty hoarder? Ask her which product from the bingo game above she uses the least. When was the last time she used it?

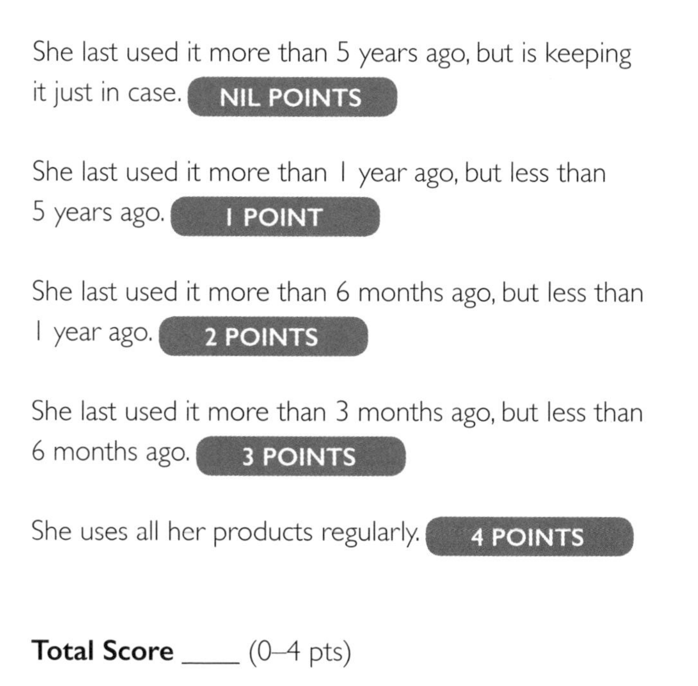

She last used it more than 5 years ago, but is keeping it just in case. **NIL POINTS**

She last used it more than 1 year ago, but less than 5 years ago. **1 POINT**

She last used it more than 6 months ago, but less than 1 year ago. **2 POINTS**

She last used it more than 3 months ago, but less than 6 months ago. **3 POINTS**

She uses all her products regularly. **4 POINTS**

Total Score ____ (0–4 pts)

Chapter Three: Scoring

Add up your score on each question to get your total score for Chapter Three, then find out how your woman measures up below.

Q1 Score ____ (0–4 pts)

Q2 Score ____ (0–10 pts)

Q3 Score ____ (0–4 pts)

Q4 Score ____ (0–16 pts)

Total Chapter Score ___ (0–34 pts)

25–34 pts: Your gal loves to look good, and you notice her! She has a style that she feels comfortable and confident wearing, and has a good awareness of the products she's using.

17–24 pts: Your gal likes to experiment with beauty, but doesn't take it too seriously. She knows what she likes, and she hopes you like it too.

9–16 pts: Your gal may occasionally go overboard with changes in her appearance or buy products that she never uses. Make sure you let her know when you think she looks beautiful. She might be trying to catch your eye.

0–8 pts: Your gal may feel insecure in the beauty department. If she's constantly changing her appearance, spending a very long time getting ready, or buying products she doesn't use, it could be a good time to remind her that she's still the girl you fell in love with.

Chapter Four

Smarty Pants

Having met and charmed the woman of your dreams into being with you, it would be nice if she could remember it. How well does your woman's memory work when it comes to the important stuff?

I Commemoration Recollection

Does your partner always remember the important stuff? Ask her to recall the following big dates. Score 1 point for each date she can remember. Feel free to substitute dates that may hold more importance to her than the ones listed below.

The anniversary of the first time you met. ☐

The anniversary of the first time you said "I love you." ☐

Your birthday. ☐

Your pet's birthday. ☐

Your best friend's birthday. ☐

Your mother's birthday. ☐

Her parents' wedding anniversary. ☐

Your parents' wedding anniversary. ☐

Total Score ____ (0–8 pts)

2 Sublime Scholar

Does your girl remember her school days—or is it more of a school daze? Give her 1 point for each of the topics in the left-hand column that she can match correctly to the lesson on the right.

1. The Theory of Relativity — **a.** Philosophy

2. Existentialism — **b.** Math

3. Chaos Theory — **c.** Physics

4. Iambic Pentameter — **d.** Literature

Total Score ____ (0–4 pts)

Answers: 1c, 2a, 3b, 4d

$E=mc^2$

3 Debate Club

A great relationship is all about healthy debates, a meeting of minds, the sharing of principles, and deep discussions that allow for learning and growth. Whether it's about politics, religion, or who left the refrigerator door open, being able to hash out facts and feelings is vital. How likely are you to win a debate (or an outright argument) with your partner?

We argue so much, no one is a winner. **NIL POINTS**

I always win debates and arguments with her, no matter what. **1 POINT**

We never argue about anything. **2 POINTS**

I have a zero percent chance of ever winning any argument with my partner. Let's just say I let her win. **3 POINTS**

If she knows more about a subject, she can convince me, and vice versa. **4 POINTS**

Total Score ____ (0–4 pts)

4 Activity: Extracurricular Interests

Does your gal have what it takes to be Number One in these extracurricular activities? There's only one way to find out. Have your lovely lady try out for each activity and see if she can make the cut! Award her between 0–4 points for her performance in each activity.

Activity	Score
Cheerleading: Show off your best dance and cheerleading moves	
Drama: Act out a dramatic scene	
Choir: Sing a song	
Track and Field: Sprint for 100 meters	
Student Body President: Give a speech	
Art: Draw or paint a picture	

Total Score ___ (0–24 pts)

Chapter Four: Scoring

Add up your score on each question to get your total score for Chapter Four, then find out how your woman measures up below.

Q1 Score ___ (0–8 pts)
Q2 Score ___ (0–4 pts)
Q3 Score ___ (0–4 pts)
Q4 Score ___ (0–24 pts)

Total Chapter Score ___ (0–40 pts)

31–40 pts: Your woman has the brains and the moves to make her "queen of the castle." You should put her knowledge to use and join a trivia team or tutor needy children.

21–30 pts: She's a whiz! Her mind is like a rusty steel trap that just needs a little polishing up.

11–20 pts: Your woman may have street smarts, but she needs to brush up on the book learning! Take a trip to the local library together, or introduce her to the Internet.

0–10 pts: Find her deeply hidden talents and celebrate them!

Chapter Five

Reality Check

Some issues just aren't black and white. Is your girl completely honest with you? Are you completely honest with her? In this chapter, find out how often she stretches the truth—or completely obliterates it.

1 Little White Lies

Does your woman value honesty or does she value kindness? These two things can be mutually exclusive, and the wrong choice can really rock the boat in your relationship. To what extent does your woman think it is OK to lie?

It is OK to lie about anything you don't want to feel bad about or get in trouble for. **NIL POINTS**

It is OK to lie to save face and protect yourself from scrutiny.
1 POINT

It is never OK to lie, ever, no matter what, even if it hurts someone's feelings. You've always got to be real.
2 POINTS

It is OK to lie to protect someone else's feelings, as long as the lie doesn't have the potential to hurt anyone.
3 POINTS

It's not OK to lie, but it is kind and acceptable to omit hurtful truths that are irrelevant. **4 POINTS**

Total Score ____ (0–4 pts)

2 Exaggeration Nation

Exaggerating isn't exactly lying, but it's not exactly telling the truth, either. Exaggerating regularly about day-to-day things can signal a lack of perspective about what's really important, or a lack of precision with language, and should be avoided whenever possible. However, if your gal never peppers her speech with hyperbole, talking to her may feel a bit like talking to a robot.

Ask her to describe her day in detail. Keep a tally of each time she exaggerates or uses hyperbole. Make sure to nod and smile the whole time to encourage her to continue for several minutes.

	Tally
Totally or completely or one-hundred percent.	_____
Something or someone is the absolute best or absolute worst.	_____
For the millionth, hundredth, or thousandth time.	_____
I love her/him to death, but …	_____
It took forever.	_____

Other exaggerations (add a tally mark for each one you catch).

If she exaggerated 9 times or more in several minutes: 0 pts.
If she exaggerated 7–8 times in several minutes: 1 pt.
If she exaggerated 5–6 times in several minutes: 2 pts.
If she exaggerated 3–4 times in several minutes: 3 pts.
If she exaggerated 0–2 times in several minutes: 4 pts.

Total Score ____ (0–4 pts)

3 Fact vs. Fiction

Does your woman really know you? Would she spot a fib of your own tucked neatly into your life story? Take a few moments to fill in the blanks with details about yourself, and then see if she can guess which events are fact and which are fiction. Award her 1 point for each answer she gets correct. Feel free to tweak the details to make it even trickier for her to unravel!

Fact/Fiction: I ran for student body president.

Fact/Fiction: ________________________________
(fill in the blank with something personal)

Fact/Fiction: I had an unusual pet when I was growing up.

Fact/Fiction: ________________________________
(fill in the blank with something personal)

Fact/Fiction: I once played video games for 24 hours straight.

Fact/Fiction: ________________________________
(fill in the blank with something personal)

Fact/Fiction: I played in a band at high school.

Fact/Fiction: ________________________________
(fill in the blank with something personal)

Total Score ____ (0–8 pts)

4 Activity: Sunny Side Up

Positive thinking is all the rage these days. Does your woman speak the language of positivity? If she can find a silver lining to these dreary incidents, she deserves a medal. Award her 0–2 points, depending on how convincing her positive take is on these terrible situations.

In the middle of winter, the plumber tells you you'll have no hot water or heat for an entire month. ☐

You and your partner both contract a very rare virus that will leave you both deaf and blind within six months. ☐

Aliens land and enslave the humans of the world. ☐

You and your partner are lost in the wilderness together. ☐

You are framed for a terrible crime and have to spend 10 years in jail. ☐

Total Score _____ (0–10 pts)

Chapter Five: Scoring

Add up your score on each question to get your total score for Chapter Five, then find out how your woman measures up below.

Q1 Score ____ (0–4 pts)
Q2 Score ____ (0–4 pts)
Q3 Score ____ (0–8 pts)
Q4 Score ____ (0–10 pts)

Total Chapter Score ____ (0–26 pts)

20–26 pts: Your gal knows how to balance truth and sniff out dishonesty. She's truthful and accurate and isn't prone to drama. Overall, a positive and trustworthy gal.

13–19 pts: She has a penchant for excitement and drama, but she usually chooses the plain and simple truth. It's just easier that way. She is mainly a glass-half-full kind of person.

7–12 pts: Your gal knows the difference between truth and lies, but it's not entirely clear whether she cares. Her glass is almost empty.

0–6 pts: It's possible that your gal feels like she may get into trouble or teased for being her honest-to-goodness self. It's also possible that she's a pathological liar.

Chapter Six

Entertainment Value

They say that the couple that plays together, stays together! Common interests can bring a couple closer and create wonderful opportunities for fun and bonding. What does your girl do for fun? Is she a homebody or a wild child? Answer the questions in this chapter and discover your partner's most entertaining qualities.

1 Fear Factor

Does a creak in the night send your woman running into your arms, or is she the type to push past her comfort zone and embrace the things that scare her? Award her 1 point for each of the scary things that she would do on this list.

Kill a spider in the house (or safely remove to the outdoors). ☐

Taste a weird-looking food she's never tried before. ☐

Be the first one on the dance floor at a friend's wedding. ☐

Choose to watch a horror movie. ☐

Travel alone to a place where she doesn't speak the language. ☐

Go sky-diving. ☐

Give a 5-minute speech to a group of coworkers or neighbors. ☐

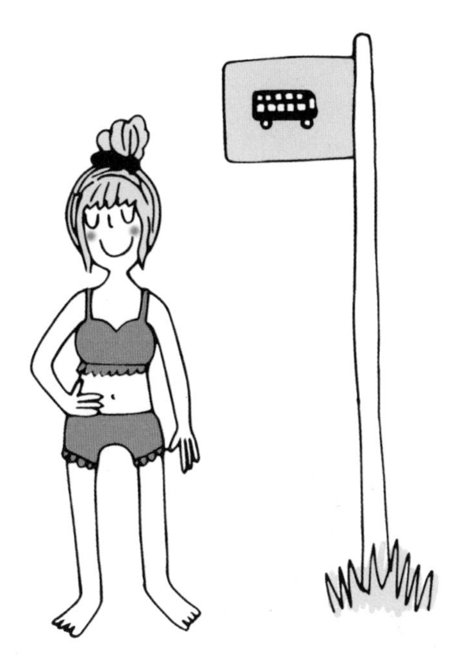

Make conversation with a total stranger. ☐

Try out for a local play. ☐

Wear a bikini in public. ☐

Total Score ____ (0–10 pts)

2 Guilty Pleasures

What secret pleasures does your woman enjoy when you're not around? Give her 1 point for each of these that she admits to (or that you know about).

Secret snacks. ☐

Inane reality TV shows. ☐

Gossip and tabloid magazines. ☐

Social media stalking. ☐

Cell phone games. ☐

Cheesy romance movies. ☐

YouTube video binging. ☐

Retail therapy (shopping for fun, not for necessity). ☐

Karaoke, lip syncing, and/or dancing it out. ☐

Other: ____________

Total Score ____ (0–10 pts)

3 To Plan or Not to Plan

"Where do you want to go?"

"I dunno, where do you want to go?"

If this conversation sounds familiar, it's time to delve deeper: are you and your gal in sync when it comes to making plans and sticking to them?

We bicker over plans—or lack thereof—all the time!

NIL POINTS

I basically have zero idea what's going on. Ever.

1 POINT

She makes all the plans, but never remembers them. It's basically a free-for-all. 2 POINTS

We have a shared calendar with everything on it and always stick to it. 3 POINTS

We make plans together and can be spontaneous together.

4 POINTS

Total Score ____ (0–4 pts)

4 In It Together

Which of these activities do you and your woman enjoy doing together, and which would you prefer to do alone? You answer first, then read the scenarios out loud to your partner. You get 1 point for each answer that is the same, and 0 points—plus some possibly awkward conversations—if your answer is different.

	You	**Her**
See a movie.	☐	☐
Go out to dinner.	☐	☐
Shoe shopping.	☐	☐
House cleaning.	☐	☐
Grocery shopping.	☐	☐
Weekend out of town.	☐	☐
Get a massage.	☐	☐
Go out dancing.	☐	☐
Watch TV.	☐	☐
Watch live music.	☐	☐

Total Score ____ (0–10 pts)

Chapter Six: Scoring

Add up your score on each question to get your total score for Chapter Six, then find out how your woman measures up below.

Q1 Score ____ (0–10 pts)
Q2 Score ____ (0–10 pts)
Q3 Score ____ (0–4 pts)
Q4 Score ____ (0–10 pts)

Total Chapter Score ____ (0–34 pts)

26–34 pts: The perfect couple pics you post on social media are actually true! You and your gal are perfectly suited.

17–25 pts: You two have a nice balance of together time and alone time. Focus on the fun and forget the rest.

8–16 pts: You don't always agree on what to do and when to do it, but when you do connect, you enjoy one another.

0–7 pts: If you must stay together, try to find at least one or two TV shows that you like to watch together and call it a happy life.

Chapter Seven

Sexy Time

Does your girl turn the lights low and your bedroom into your very own private, adult-themed fantasy land? Or does her finest lingerie look more like sweatpants? Turn up the slow jams, because things are about to get hot. Or not. How does your woman score in the Sexy Time category?

1 In the Mood For Love

You're in the mood for love, but is your partner? Which of these best describes your romantic chemistry in the bedroom?

She makes excuses to avoid intimacy like a magician pulls a rabbit out of a hat. **NIL POINTS**

She's very aggressive. I have a hard time keeping up. **1 POINT**

We schedule "date nights" (wink wink) at least once a month and stick to the plan most of the time. **2 POINTS**

We read each other's signals well—I can tell when she's in the mood and vice versa. **3 POINTS**

Basically our relationship is like fireworks exploding for both of us all the time. **4 POINTS**

Total Score ____ (0–4 pts)

2 For Work or For Play?

You've got to heat up the oven before you bake bread ... Different women have different turn ons, and being able to push your woman's buttons is a huge part of a satisfying sex life. Give your girl 1 point for each item on this list that could reasonably be considered foreplay in your household.

Playing a certain artist or album. ☐

Lighting candles or incense. ☐

Doing dishes or other chores while your partner relaxes. ☐

Reading or reciting poetry to one another. ☐

Massages: feet, back, hand, or all of the above. ☐

Going for a romantic walk under a full moon. ☐

Going shopping for something sparkly. ☐

Sharing a delicious dessert. ☐

Peeping at some naughty pictures or reading about some exciting encounters. ☐

Whispering something suggestive into her ear. ☐

Total Score ____ (0–10 pts)

3 Spicing It Up

Remember how sexy things were when you first met? Now forget it! Sorry to be the bearer of bad news, but a serious relationship is a long game, and those hormone-fueled days are over pretty quickly. The good news? The trust and affection you develop over time allows you to get way freakier than you did in the early days. Give your girl 1 point for each of the things she might be willing to try. Feel free to cross out these suggestions and write in your own.

PDA (public displays of affection). ☐

Role play. Is that the pizza delivery boy knocking? ☐

A little spanking (also known as 50 Shades of Fun). ☐

A visit to an adult "book" store. (PS—they sell more than books.) ☐

Strip poker. Or strip Scrabble. Your choice. ☐

Whipped cream, chocolate sauce, and a cherry on top. ☐

A secret rendezvous at a crowded party. ☐

Creams, oils, lotions, or gels. Flavored or original recipe. ☐

Ménage à trois. ☐

Blindfold. ☐

Total Score ____ (0–10 pts)

4 You Dog, You

Which animal is your woman most like in the bedroom?

A slug. **NIL POINTS**

A porcupine. Ouch! **1 POINT**

Pegasus. Beautiful and surprising in unexpected ways. **2 POINTS**

A cute and curious monkey. **3 POINTS**

An exotic jungle cat, sleek and a little scary. **4 POINTS**

Total Score ____ (0–4 pts)

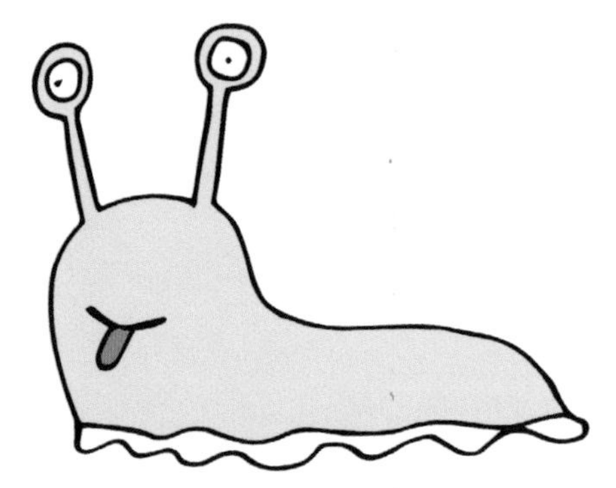

Chapter Seven: Scoring

Add up your score on each question to get your total score for Chapter Seven, then find out how your woman measures up below.

Q1 Score ____ (0–4 pts)
Q2 Score ____ (0–10 pts)
Q3 Score ____ (0–10 pts)
Q4 Score ____ (0–4 pts)

Total Chapter Score ____ (0–28 pts)

22–28 pts: Red hot! You two have so much chemistry you might blow up the lab.

15–21 pts: Your gal has romance running deep within her veins. Wake it up with a little romantic gesture of your own.

7–14 pts: It's not easy to keep the romance alive during busy day-to-day life. Keep trying to initiate a little affection and you may find that your woman's romance score improves.

0–6 pts: Platonic relationships have a long and mostly successful history, right? Here's hoping.

Chapter Eight

Communication Revelations

Communication within a relationship might come through loud and clear, or it might be full of static and get completely lost in translation. How do you and your partner communicate when it comes to the big issues, the small stuff, and everything in between?

1 Speaking My Language

Is your gal fluent in bloke-speak? If she can distil the meaning out of these "everyday" phrases, you're halfway toward the open, honest communication that makes a relationship worthwhile. Read a phrase from the left-hand column, and then the possible answers from the column on the right, and score your gal 1 point for each correct answer.

1. I'm just going to go out and grab one with the boys.

2. Why don't you watch it and tell me how it is?

3. You may not want to go in there right away.

4. The game's on tonight.

5. I'm putting my foot down.

6. I was just kidding!

7. You look so hot in that dress.

a. Can we go now?

b. I'll probably see you tomorrow morning and I'll probably be feeling pretty bad.

c. I'd love to hang out with you, but I'll be watching TV.

d. It really smells bad in there and I'm embarrassed.

e. That looks so boring.

f. Please? Pretty please?

g. Oops, I said something stupid.

Total Score ____ (0–7 pts)

Answers: 1b, 2e, 3d, 4c, 5f, 6g, 7a

2 Intimacy Issues

Some women are more open than others when it comes to discussing their worries and fears. Some are a little too open and share every single thing that goes through their mind. How far does your woman share her innermost feelings?

My gal tells me about everything, including bathroom stuff. Enough said. Seriously. **NIL POINTS**

My gal rarely talks about her feelings—except when she's mad at me. **1 POINT**

My gal talks constantly about other people and what they did or said. Not always sure what she wants me to do about it. **2 POINTS**

My gal waits until she's frustrated to start talking, but when she does we're able to connect and talk about what's happening in her life. **3 POINTS**

My gal tells me what's on her mind and shares her thoughts about work, friends, and family—and she lets me talk about what's on my mind as well. **4 POINTS**

Total Score ____ (0–4 pts)

3 Smoke Signals

How on earth did people communicate before text messaging? Many couples text, email, direct message, and tweet each other all day long. Award your girl 1 point for each method she uses to communicate with you when you're not together.

Phone calls. ☐

Texts. ☐

Snapchat (wink wink). ☐

Video chat, Skype, or FaceTime. ☐

IMs. ☐

Emails. ☐

Letters in the mail. ☐

Secret notes. ☐

Deliveries, like flowers or candies. ☐

Messages passed through a friend, relative, or coworker. ☐

Total Score ____ (0–10 pts)

4 Activity: The Look

Partners often develop wordless forms of communication and can speak volumes with the simple lift of an eyebrow. Ask your gal to communicate something to you without saying a word and see if you can translate.

Your partner should write down what she's trying to communicate in the left-hand column and your guess in the next column. If you guess her message correctly, award her 2 points. If you get the general gist, award her 1 point. If you can't begin to guess her intentions, she gets the big zero.

Your Partner's Secret Message	**Your Guess**	**Points**
E.g. You really screwed up this time.	E.g. Want to make out?	0–2
1.		
2.		
3.		
4.		
5.		

Total Score ____ (0–10 pts)

Chapter Eight: Scoring

Add up your score on each question to get your total score for Chapter Eight, then find out how your woman measures up below.

Q1 Score ____ (0–7 pts)
Q2 Score ____ (0–4 pts)
Q3 Score ____ (0–10 pts)
Q4 Score ____ (0–10 pts)

Total Chapter Score ____ (0–31 pts)

24–31 pts: Communication is golden! You and your partner have a strong connection and can talk through even the craziest issues with grace and understanding.

16–23 pts: To rev up your communication skills, you just need to practice a little. Bring up a controversial subject and see how long you can discuss it without reverting to name-calling and foot-stomping.

8–15 pts: Talking louder and slower probably won't work this time. Your communication needs some repair work. Starting to actually listen is a good first step.

0–7 pts: Yeah, you probably need a safe word for day-to-day communication.

Chapter Nine

A Sporting Chance

You and your gal are on the same team, but are you playing the same sport? In this chapter, answer the questions and see if you and your gal are game, set, and match, or if it's a fumble every time.

1 Healthy Competition

Do you and your woman collaborate or compete? A little competition can be fun and healthy, but if you're at each other's throats, your relationship might feel intense. Which of these activities sounds most like your relationship?

An extreme cage fighting match. **NIL POINTS**

Soccer. We will go to any length to get one past each other. **1 POINT**

Tennis. We have fun batting ideas back and forth, though sometimes it gets heated. **2 POINTS**

Baseball. We take turns going in to bat, but we always come back home. **3 POINTS**

Golf. Our relationship is a hole in one! **4 POINTS**

Total Score ____ (0–4 pts)

2 The Gloves Are Off

Many people speak in sporting metaphors. Can your gal match these common metaphors with their sport?

1. We need a level playing field.	**a.** Golf
2. He's a real heavyweight.	**b.** Tennis
3. I got the deal—won it hands down.	**c.** Football
4. The ball's in your court.	**d.** Boxing
5. Bullseye. You got it.	**e.** Baseball
6. Sometimes life throws you a curveball.	**f.** Horse racing
7. His performance has really been below par lately.	**g.** Darts or archery

Total Score ____ (0–7 pts)

Answers: 1c, 2d, 3f, 4b, 5g, 6e, 7a

3 Get in the Game

They say that couples who workout together live longer and are healthier. Which of these athletic activities would your partner agree to do with you? Award her 1 point for each sport she'd try.

Jogging. ☐

Running a marathon. ☐

Swimming. ☐

Racquetball or squash. ☐

Soccer. ☐

Boxing or kickboxing. ☐

Yoga. ☐

Biking. ☐

Dancing. ☐

Volleyball. ☐

Total Score ____ (0–10 pts)

4 Activity: Three-Pointer

It's a slam dunk! Can your girl score against you? Set up a "goal" using a trash can or bucket, and see if your girl can get a balled-up piece of paper past you and into the goal. Give her three chances. Award her 3 points if she gets it in cleanly, 2 points if she has to sneak it in, 1 point if she "almost" gets it in, and zero points if she has no chance!

Round 1: ___ pts (0–3 pts)
Round 2: ___ pts (0–3 pts)
Round 3: ___ pts (0–3 pts)

Total Score ____ (0–9 pts)

Chapter Nine: Scoring

Add up your score on each question to get your total score for Chapter Nine, then find out how your woman measures up below.

Q1 Score ____ (0–4 pts)
Q2 Score ____ (0–7 pts)
Q3 Score ____ (0–10 pts)
Q4 Score ____ (0–9 pts)

Total Chapter Score ____ (0–30 pts)

26–30 pts: You and your gal maintain a healthy level of competition and are up for trying anything—as long as it's together. YOLO!

18–25 pts: You and your gal are in the same ballpark and can really hit a homerun when it comes to sports. Or insert your own favorite sporting metaphor here and keep on running for the finish line!

9–17 pts: You and your gal don't really see eye-to-eye on the whole sports thing. So what? Unless you're referring to the bedroom Olympics, are sports really that big a factor in a happy relationship?

0–8 pts: You neither speak the same sporting language nor enjoy the same activities—no worries, sports are only the world's favorite pastime. You'll certainly find something else to do with all your free time. Like knitting.

Chapter Ten

Bringing Home the Bacon (and Frying It Too)

Your woman can do anything. She can juggle work, home, family, friends, and she can stay cool as a cucumber while she does it. Answer the questions in this chapter to discover how you can lend a hand—or maybe just clear the way for your woman to do her thing!

I Working the System

Enjoying your work can bring joy to your whole life, while an unsatisfying job can ripple into other parts of your life, even your relationship. Which answer best describes how your girl feels about her work?

She considers her job to be literal torture. **NIL POINTS**

She can get through the day, but needs about an hour of uninterrupted quiet time to soothe her rage. **1 POINT**

She works to earn a living, but has no problem leaving her work behind. **2 POINTS**

She enjoys work a little too much—one might say that she's obsessed! **3 POINTS**

She is making her career dreams come true, and it's awesome to watch. **4 POINTS**

Total Score ____ (0–4 pts)

2 The Last Day of Work

Do you and your woman daydream about the day you can leave the working world behind and spend every day pursuing your hobbies and relaxing? Give your girl 1 point for each of the retirement activities that she'd probably agree to pursue with you on that fine day.

Travel. ☐

Art or photography classes. ☐

Spend time with friends. ☐

Play golf. ☐

Work on your home. ☐

Garden. ☐

Do volunteer work. ☐

Go fishing. ☐

Read the classics. ☐

Write a novel or memoir. ☐

Total Score ____ (0–10 pts)

3 The Best Things in Life Are Free

Does your girl have expensive tastes, or can she make a dollar stretch? Which of the answers below best describes her spending style?

Legally, she's been diagnosed as a high-level shopaholic. **NIL POINTS**

She uses shopping as a form of therapy, and she seems to need a lot of therapy. **1 POINT**

She likes nice things, but tries to balance her spending by saving in other areas. **2 POINTS**

She finds happiness outside of material possessions, and is basically a budget goddess. **3 POINTS**

Total Score ____ (0–3 pts)

4 Activity: The Price is Right

Who handles the bills in your household? If you pay the electricity, water, and power bills, see if your gal can guess how much each item costs. If she pays the bills, quiz her on how much your favorite lunch items and your haircut cost, or how much that new cell phone you've been eyeing might run you. If she comes within $1, award her 2 points. If she comes within $5, award her 1 point. If she's way off, she gets zero points.

Actual Cost	Your Partner's Guess	Points (0–2 pts)
1.		
2.		
3.		
4.		
5.		
6.		

Total Score _____ (0–12 pts)

Chapter Ten: Scoring

Add up your score on each question to get your total score for Chapter Ten, then find out how your woman measures up below.

Q1 Score ____ (0–4 pts)
Q2 Score ____ (0–10 pts)
Q3 Score ____ (0–3 pts)
Q4 Score ____ (0–12 pts)

Total Chapter Score ____ (0–29 pts)

23–29 pts: You and your gal are open and honest about work and finances. Keep up the good work, and support each other as you follow your dreams through your careers and into retirement.

15–22 pts: Your gal is on a great path to career fulfilment and retirement heaven. Make sure you support her and take on your share of the work around the house so she can do what she needs to do.

7–14 pts: Careers change over time. Encourage your gal to take up hobbies or change her career path if she's not getting enough satisfaction on a daily basis.

0–6 pts: If your gal is unhappy in her work, with her finances, and with the idea of retirement fun, it's probably time to figure out what else might be wrong—and fix it. That's a lot of unhappiness to carry every day.

Total Score

Write up all your scores over the ten chapters and add them together before reading the final results below.

	SCORE
Chapter One (0–42 pts)	
Chapter Two (0–28 pts)	
Chapter Three (0–23 pts)	
Chapter Four (0–40 pts)	
Chapter Five (0–26 pts)	
Chapter Six (0–34 pts)	
Chapter Seven (0–28 pts)	
Chapter Eight (0–31 pts)	
Chapter Nine (0–30 pts)	
Chapter Ten (0–29 pts)	
Total Score (0–311 pts)	

IF SHE SCORED VERY HIGH

235–311 pts

You always knew your gal was the best, but now you have actual numerical proof. You and your woman share a deep connection—possibly even an otherworldly bond. You two will be together forever, and still be very much in love when you are old and gray. Your gal is so awesome that if she dies before you, she will come back and haunt you just so you guys can keep hanging out together, forever! Yes, your gal is a keeper. She loves and supports you, and the feeling is mutual.

IF SHE SCORED HIGH

157–234 pts

Your gal's score shows that she has what it takes to be a wonderful life partner, best friend, and lover. Whatever you take on together, from skydiving to watching movies at home, you can just relax and enjoy your relationship with total trust that your partner has your back. Watch out, though, your friendships might actually be in trouble because you can't help but stare at your woman with puppy dog eyes and spout romantic lyrics like you're an 80s rock star singing a love ballad. Try to keep your feelings under wraps when you're in public, but make sure you let your lady know how much you appreciate her.

IF SHE SCORED MEDIUM

79–156 pts

Your gal is not your average lady, is she? She's like a rare orchid growing in the wild. When she blooms, it's breathtaking and you feel lucky to be witness to such a miracle, but if you do one little thing wrong—that's it. You can try to improve the conditions, you can shield her from the weather, but one false step and it's game over. That doesn't mean you should stop trying, though. On the off-chance you get your orchid to bloom, you will live the rest of your life a happy man.

IF SHE SCORED LOW

0–78 pts

There are many, many romances that end in tragedy, as yours likely will. *Romeo and Juliet* is perhaps the most famous, but there are others. Like the blockbuster movie *Titanic*. So make sure you and your gal take in all the beautiful ocean views and the fun onboard the ship of your relationship, because the sad truth is that unless you get back on course, you're headed straight for an iceberg.